Pain In Paradise The Poetry Book

By
Marianna
Drunnamanio

Table of contents

Pain in paradise

Amazing how
something that
Feels so good can
hurt. It can rain all
day but you know at
one point the sun
will shine and you
forget anything ever
got wet. Why do we
crave things that
are toxic for us?
Like a drug.
Obviously it isn't
good for you but we
love the feeling no
matter the after
effects. That's just
life. Cliche but
reality. There's no
light without
darkness, you can't
appreciate
happiness without
being sad , no peace
without war, no
optimism without
being pessimistic.
Appreciate not only
the good things but
also the bad , new
experiences and
lessons mold you
into who you are.
This World is your

oyster, your
emotions are your
stepping stone,
your drive is your
tool. Use everything
to your advantage,
adapt.
With pain comes
paradise, you're
already in.
This is Pain in
paradise.

Intimacy

Intimacy.
Two connected
souls desire to
deliver sheer
Ecstasy,
beginning with a
passionate touch,
it doesn't take
much,
gripping the sheets,
clenching my feet ,
I'm addicted.
Love and affection
risen to its peak,
can't help but be a
freak,
exploring exploding
euphoria.
I'm amazed on how
the body
intertwines, leave a
mark on what's
mine,
territorial.
To be the only one
who feels your
erection as it grows,
how to make me
shake
uncontrollably only
you know,
intercourse.
Mouth to mouth,

Body to body it
takes two,
a feeling to crave,
be brave, let's try
something new.
Giving oral pleasure
staying in tune with
my tongue just to
hear the music of
your moans while
the rising of the
sun. Returning the
favor slurping my
succulent juices,
give it a taste,
a meal not to waste,
common courtesy.
InSync as I ride,
look into his eyes,
in me he resides .
A wonderful
sensation,
a man's ejaculation,
a women's satisfied
temptation,
infatuation.
Exhaustion from
climax,
sore from body
impact,
suddenly I snap
back, it was just a
flashback,
masturbation.

R.I.D.E

My life is on a ride,
the good and the
bad always
coincides, Wishing
you can fly so high
in the sky to a place
where no worries
lie. It's a scary ride.
More afraid of time,
it goes by with a
blink of an eye.
What do I rely on
when everything
and everyone is
gone ? Nothing lasts
long, beautiful
music but such a
short song. When it
all goes wrong this
ride is at it's low,
don't let no one
know that it's a
heavy load, don't let
the unhappiness
unfold, just a bump
in the road. Ride. It's
finally at its peak
stay in your seat it'll
drop at any moment
it's your job to hold
it, please don't move

life is going so
smooth stop the
pessimistic
thoughts and simply
Relax It'll DieDown
Eventually.

R.I.D.E

Eco friendly

Energy. It's the
mercury retrograde
tonight that gave
me the inspo to
write, Our universe
depends on yours
don't ignore, the
auras. Intuitions are
signs to look in
between the lines,
look deeper as if
into another
dimension,
meditation to
relieve all tension.
Breathe. Give love
get love from above.
Send hate it
retaliates, choose
your fate. We die
then revive with the
same soul , different
destiny,
déjà vu they call it?
No. It was destined
to be . The earth
was designed for
our benefit, learn to
take care of it , as
you do yourself . My
dreams are
futuristic paths or a
meaningful lessons,

my mind can only
take so much where
do I put the rest in ?
the stars only get
you so far then no
more direction,
there's no space for
mistakes We need
correction.

Rose

Red.
The color of love, the shade
of pain like blood dripping
from its veins. Strengthens
thy roots which is why the
rose shall remain, the
strongest of all plants. It's
everlasting bloom gazing
petal to petal needing no
sunshine nor rain, for she is
that rose. Standing tall,
beautiful, aroma as fulfilling
as her presence, her
existence is enough to
evolve one simple flower
into a garden. Despite the
night the seasons change.
When her Unique leaves
start to shrivel, Ice cold
stomata, breathtaking at it's
finest form. The
disintegration under the
moonlight reflects off the
wind that carries you
around proving that
everything that glitters is
not gold but for she is still
that beautiful red rose.

Double standard

Men have so much
expectations, women have
no voice. Boulders on
gentlemen shoulders, ladies
we don't have a choice.
Commend all mothers,
frown upon all the absent
fathers with no recognition
to the present ones, no
intentions of the little
blessing just wanted some
fun now he's on the run,
less of a man.
Conversations on womens
manipulation, use of the
child for revenge causes all
frustration, less of a
woman. Men have sexual
intercourse and get their
numbers up like its a game
but god forbid a female
does the same automatic
slut shame, double
standard. False convictions
towards innocent males
currently doing time in jail,
all because she said he did.
Lets say thats accurate, To
question the clothing she

had on her back regardless she didn't ask for that, as a matter of fact it hurts, to not be able to walk down the street with your favorite fucking skirt, because they said so ,yet no means no? Heres a thought, being gay is okay when its females but when its men its not, saying "im not with the gay shit" like its something to not be proud of , love is love. Double standard. Despite hormones women can overly feel, shed tears, express depression. Men refuse cause it's "weak" so they hide their stress in. Males can have friends of the opposite sex with nothing attached, but when a female does the same the assumption of sexual intercourse flows through the brain as if that's a fact, why is that? Cut the double standards.

Glass half empty

Frustration at my
procrastination,
They didn't tell us life will
be this tough,
Always feeling as though we
never do enough, give up.
Then what? You are the
chosen one, misfortunes
comes you face them don't
run. One day you're
beautiful one day not, one
day the world is yours one
days you want it to stop,
Kill the pessimism before it
starts, the proof is in your
beating heart. W.a.y.s (why
aren't you smiling) You're
not alone you just feel
lonely, pace yourself your
time comes slowly, Roof
over your head food on the
table, lifes not perfect but
it's pretty stable, don't be
ungrateful. Life
only gets harder but you've
gotta get stronger, strong
enough to make it any
longer, not only for yourself
but for everyone else.
Broken hearts and
disappointments you'll get

plenty in due time, don't
stress or live with regret
you'll be fine, debt
skyrocket, bills colliding
what's new, if money can't
buy happiness then pay up
the rents due, but genuine
love is priceless , it's all you
got when you're feeling
lifeless.
Don't know what to believe,
don't know who to believe
in, no religion but prioritize
meditation, learn yourself
for yourself, self evaluation.

This is goodbye

This is goodbye
Dont not rewind
Dismissed i leave this
behind
Speak Devious lies
Poison and deceive my
mind
Your Jealousy is a
possessing kind
Eat the fruits of our labor
And you leave me the rine
Problems occurs you switch
up on the dime
Even the worst relationship
can work over time
Yet, splitting us up is the
work of something divine.
Don't save face trying to
save pride
If your upset then go cry
Humility cannot hide
I didn't mean to go pry
Can't help if you can't rely
On me to help you fly
You know you cannot deny
I'm yours and you are mine.
You know you cannot deny
On me to help you fly
Can't help if you can't rely
Didn't mean to go pry
Humility cannot hide

If your upset then go cry
Don't save face trying to
save pride
Us splitting up was the
work of the divine
Even the worst
relationships can work over
time
Problems occur then you go
switch up on the dime
You eat the fruits of our
labors and you left me the
rine
Your jealousy is a
possessing kind
Poison and deceive my
mind
Speak Devious lies
Dismissed, I leave this
behind
Dont not rewind
This is goodbye.

- Sherman Wilson Jr.

LIVID

Didn't you think I needed
that heart to live?
This love was already so
hard to give. Commitment
is what you lack. Tell me
everything I want to hear to
then be wack, and have the
nerve to try to come back.
Take a step back please, as
a matter of fact get on your
knees and pray to god you'll
find another woman like
me. LIVID.
I wish your mother taught
you how to cherish a
female, seems like true love
only happens in fairy tales.
It'll never change my
loyalty, I don't need
someone's love, I want
someone to love me with

me. Is that too much to ask?
Wanted it to last but now
it's the past, our history is
history, it isn't
a mystery. True colors
come out like water in a
hamper, you just wanted to
tamper, then when I leave
cry like a baby someone
pass this man a pamper. But
on a serious note you are a
fool, women aren't
disposable nor are we a
tool. Ignorance is bliss. But
it's nothing new, men want
their cake and eat it too.
LIVID.
No goals nor ambitions yet
mind set on wealth, how did
I expect you to care about
me when you don't even
care about yourself? Your
words were the cure but
your eyes told the lies.
Unloyalty has never and will

never be wise. Love to play
games, time out, you're
benched now but somehow
you still ran the clock
meanwhile wishing
someone can shoot their
shot. Time isn't to be
wasted neither is energy,
validation that you just
wasn't meant for me.
LIVID.
You gave her what we had
in private, confront you and
then you stay silent. I told
you things you didn't
deserve to know, this shit
so unfortunate but it's
helping me grow. I gave
you all of me but it wasn't
enough guess to you I'm
just the diamond in the ruff.
I don't need that though
which is why I called it
quits, Karmas a bitch.
Instant message.. Late

reply. Saying goodbye. Now look who's LIVID.

No orgasms

How can you crave
something you
never felt before?
Disappointment
galore,
All the sign you can
not ignore,
Sex shouldn't be
this much of a bore
Do more.
Don't know if I came
cause you don't ask
The first round you
can barely even last
In the past you said
I was gonna tap out
But all the freak talk
was just for clout,
Cut it out.
Foreplay is trash
always rushing it,
make my femine
parts want to say
forget it , making
me want to be
celibate.
It's more than just
penetration,

sometimes I just use
my imagination, just
to get some
satisfaction, gotta
end it with some
masturbation. 66
percent of females
fake orgasms in the
USA sad to say, give
you your nut to get
it out the way.
That's not okay . It
begins with the
soul, have sex with
the mind,
passionate
aggression. Be
rough but kind. But
a man like that is so
hard to find.
Selfishly satisfy your
selflessness so a
majority of women
think it's a myth .
Just check the stats.
Orgasm? What is
that?

Tsunami

Tsunami, that's your
nickname.
I know most want to ride
your wave

With their surfboards
I only seen the surface and
know your worth more

Seductive, yet destructive if
fucked with
Cliffhanger....

Hello, my name is stranger
Sense the sensation of
danger
Of new interactions
Don't treat this like a
distraction

Right now the slightest
attraction
Could have us both doing
backflips

Tsunami
I'll embrace you kamikaze
Come rampant

Send your waves

Knock weaker ones astray
Yet on our path I stay
This is our dance
Yet the music hasn't begun
to play.

-Sherman Wilson Jr.

She is me

She does not have a happy
soul, people fold , apples
are gold with the blackest
core, the skin you tore to
see a glimpse of the inside ,
its in her mind let's unwind
and rewind to the time you
said everything will be fine ,
optimism keeps one steady
while pessimism keeps one
ready. People change like
the seasons but everything
happens for a reason, she
does not dwell say your
goodbyes take all your lies
hope you got a rise, but

rise to this, someone you'll miss, she was the was the greatest gift. She is pure a different breed, something you'll need. A different vibe you'll crave on your worst days, but still not amazed. She asks why, if she tries to give her all to then fall for the red flags you pretend you don't have I guess it's sad but She kinda glad that She knows now. She is in tune with her intuition her happiness is her mission, but when the stars glisten who's there to listen to the stories of her universe it's a gift and a curse . She is a great friend the loyalty doesn't end but she will not mend the broken bonds you send, when it's all said and done just know she had fun, but a new chapter has just

begun, it was destined. She
is careful with who she
keeps around, analyzes who
doesn't make a sound to her
music that makes her who
she is, the reason she still
lives, her purpose.
Set her free.
She is me .

Dear mama

You are my blessing ,
I can't imagine a world
without you. It's like trying
to remember someone you
never knew.
Even when you had nothing
you gave us everything and
I will not stop until I can
repay what you've done for
me, but honestly , that
won't be enough I wish I
can carry all your worries
so your life won't be so
rough.
You are beautiful, you are
strong, you are
independent, if you were on
your last dime you would
still let me lend it .
That shoulder you let me
cry on only strengthens are
connection, might not take
all your advice but I know
you point me in the right
direction.

Despite our fights and your
insights you just might, be
the person I'll cherish until I
see the light.
I try to put it in words but
it's hard to explain just
know
I love you more than life
itself and that will remain.
You are appreciated .

Who knew

I'm scared too.
To give your all and
dedicate your life to
another's soul for them to
fold leave you with no one
to hold, who knew. Who
knew that every time you
meet someone else, your
walls are higher than after
the blunt you smoked to get
rid of the pain you felt.
Convinced that being single
is better so you leave your
guard up, but you're tired of
the quick fucks, I know it
sucks but make your mind
up. What is life without risk
you never know unless you
do, but you won't allow that
side of you. Trust issues?
Basically. But I remember

what every man did to me
and there will never be a
day where I'll let their
mistakes determine how my
faith will be nor my loyalty.
Society says love at first
sight but I say love until you
can get it right . There's
plenty of baby showers and
not enough weddings, same
situations, different person
and setting. You want to
love and be loved but "no
ones here for the long run"
such a strict prediction.,
just a walking contradiction.
Tell me stories about your
past how it all didn't last ,
absurd to know that's
there's females taking good
men for granted and we're
running out of those, cause
I don't remember the last
time a man has ever gotten
me a fucking rose, but

forget the flowers I want
your hours, but once you
get to liking you explain
relationships like it's a myth
or some sort of magical
power. Imagine liking
someone and not wanting
to, it's like working a 9 to 5
like the rent is due, do what
you have to do, to survive.
Can see the beautiful fear in
your eyes, take a second to
realize, I'm scared too.
Who knew.

Body parts

Hand in hand,
with every touch creates
energy that feels as though
we were meant to be
connected to light up the
universe.
Lips to lips,
I can taste your beautiful
vocals while smelling the
wonderful aroma of your
soul. My tastebuds crave
your aura. I am deaf to any
music that is not your own.
Fascinated by your
rhythmic tones. Speaks
volumes.
Chest to chest,

we're in sync with every
heartbeat a melody that
seems to be only meant for
me .
Arm in arm,
we are in separable no one
can do any harm until the
day that you let go. So I'll
hold on like our lives
depended on it. So you will
never have the chance.
Face to face,
even Picasso isn't capable of
a masterpiece such as
yourself. As though angels
carved every feature into
perfection. Every crease
every mark every wrinkle
was meant to be admired
and appreciated every
second, and that is exactly
why I will remain to do so.
We are one.
Conjoined from our
fingertips to the tips of our

toes we will continue to
walk this earth... together...
for eternity.

REASON

I am poor with the richest soul the richest ambition the richest family money can not buy, I refuse to stay middle class until the day that I die, I do not crave a lifetime of 9 to 5s . But we all have to start somewhere.....but not all over, overwhelmed and clouded by the worries of tomorrow so of course it's hard to stay sober. Humble yourself every second of everyday, just as fast as it came it can all quickly be taken away. I've been through alot, from not having a dime for a meal, to homelessness, even having to bathe with hot water in a pot, three jobs although my goal oriented ambition never stops, it's just more of a reason.
What have you done for yourself?

What have you done for
your mental health?
The partying, drinking,
smoking, what are you
celebrating? It's just a short
term fix it doesn't really
help. But you still make it a
priority if not you're
depressed. Tried to give it a
rest, try to do what's best ,
don't know what to do next.
Where's the party at?
Intoxication only
strengthens the caged
negative thoughts piercing
my brain asking myself
what is my purpose, will
this life stay the same? I no
longer feel sane, I am at war
with self doubt, I think it's
time to find a new route,
just another reason.
The way I look at life now is
we were all put on this
earth for a reason which is
why we can adapt and
evolve. Everything is
destined so leave the things
that we can not control for
the high power to solve.
Repeat after me. I am
strong. I am beautiful. I am
capable. I am here. And with
those things alone... is my
reason.

9

Back to 2009
That's twelve years of age
Even then moved like stoics
Felt somewhat like a mage
But all of the progression
Could be atone to the
blessing
I received at conception
Not even god could
intercept it
I'm fucking life raw without
the contraceptive
Guess I'm stupid but that's
a matter of perspective
You can fuck your life up in
a matter of seconds
Flash forward
That's my only path of
direction
My birth right my path that
is destined

And I don't care I'll move
with discretion
Take the curses and the
blessing
Can't have one without the
other
Like a child with no mother
I don't fly bitch I hover
I ascend at my own grind
Being debt free is a blessing
gives me a piece of mind
And I did it with the nine to
five.
Aint gone kie
you know the kid a to hustle
on the side.
And a nigga never had to
keep a nine.

- Sherman Wilson Jr.

Now she had just self expressed herself to death now nothing's left, knows her worth but it is still not enough to be kept. Is it me and my toxic traits and playing the victim? Or is it him and all the broken promises that kept me with him. Pick my brain feel my pain, hear to listen not only to respond, maintain an unbreakable bond. Inseparable like Velcro although distant in my mental. Confusion, needing clarity, reassurance is everything, provide it to me. He loves me, he loves me not. He loves me then he stops. I miss him, he does not. I want him but I can not. “I’m not going anywhere” but you left. “I want you in my life “ yeah I bet . You’re the little boy with his brand new toy gets bored sticks it in his treasure chest. 2 weeks or maybe two years you come back shed a couple tears, I take you back with the same fear. That night was so emotional, didn’t know what I was supposed to do. Gave me the answer to my question but I already knew. Intuition. Realized what he was missing . Imagine all the things you did with her I do with another man. I can forgive things like that I’m used to it but I doubt you can . Feel myself slowly getting distant, said you’re trying there’s a possibility I could’ve missed it . But

don't try just do ,
frustrations determining
what's a lie and what is
true. Weak, vulnerable,
naive, what I see when I'm
looking outside back at me .
Can't be mad at myself. I
love that man with my
whole heart but I'm not
going to continue to let this
continue to tear me apart.
When it's good it's great,
when it's bad it was a
mistake , to you at least.
God forbid I tell you how I
feel I released the beast .
Now I'm the bad guy. I'm
the reason why we never
get along. I'm the one who's
always in the wrong but am
I wrong for loving you am I
wrong for taking you back
every time? For wanting
you to be mines ? You don't
see a future but I'll do

anything to get it, but if you
don't see a future why
should I stress shit.
Constantly deciding on
which way to turn ,
regardless of whether I go
left or right I'll always learn.

Abstract souls

We are not color
coordinated
We can not fill in the lines
But our shape still coincides
Constant binding
constantly correlate
Which creates an art
A beautiful piece of
madness
But not so picture perfect
But it's worth it
Brighter paints make for
brighter days
Shade away no pain of the
imperfections
Erase no mistake
Use it to Create.
Calms the mental state.
You.
Me.
Abstract souls.

Proudly

This red lipstick makes me a
puta
I'll wear it proudly.
These fishnets make me a
hoe.
I'll wear it proudly.
I'm too fat for skinny's
I'll wear it proudly
I should rock my natural
hair
I'll wear this wig proudly
These long nails make me
ghetto
I'll wear them proudly
The crop tops show my
muffin top
I'll wear and show it proudly
This cleavage makes me
look easy
But I'll show them proudly
These piercings and tattoos
make me look demonic
I'll get more proudly

Swearing makes me ugly
I don't give two fucks I'll
keep it up proudly
Makeup is for the insecure?
I'll still apply it proudly
No matter what you do in
life there's always an
ignorant opinion. Continue
to be you.
Proudly.

CHEATERS

Why?
Why lie?
Why hide?
Why watch me cry?
You couldn't just be mature
and tell me I am no longer
what you crave. I look in the
mirror thinking, what do I
lack? What can I do to get
him back?
Fuck that .
I was loyal, I told you
everything , gave my all for
you to give it to the next
bitch, I meant female, no
disrespect but then again
did she know about me? Is
she oblivious or just a
sneaky trick? It's none of
my concern anymore she

can have that community
dick.
I will never put someone
through this type of pain, I'll
break things off and do
things conscience free but
you didn't care enough to
do that for me so I'll let it
be. But I can't help the fact
that now I'm protective of
my heart you ever so
slightly tore apart. The
heart I try so hard to mend
together myself everyday
another man tried to come
my way. You don't deserve
to be on my mind all the
time whether it's something
that reminds me of you or
helps me despise you.
Because of you I am not
ready to give my all,
because of you I question
my appearance and
mannerisms. Because of

you I overly apologize and don't believe a thing anyone says to me . All promises are bound to be broken as well as everything else. This isn't me.

....

Woke up one morning and instantly, I wasn't sad anymore. I thank god for that strength and also relieving me from things that aren't meant for me. I take it as a lesson now. I can love as if I've never been hurt. I love myself enough to not rely on anyone else's. I'm glowing again. I smile brighter, I feel healthy. I am myself again. So that game you tried to play is over. Disqualification of a Cheater.

Women empowerment

God's best creation was us.
you cannot say otherwise
we create populations,
nurture and supply.
Although we are emotional,
it doesn't mean we are weak
nor that we are not capable
of independence . We are
the strongest of beings, our
hearts are big enough to
share , strive big enough to
motivate, cortex big enough
to overpass the sexist one
sided minds that really
believe we are not queens,
that we shouldn't be treated
as royalty rather than a
housewife society expects,
that we are good for
nothing but our cooks and
looks, that we can not do
the things men can do and
even better. That we can

not make a choice , that we can not make a stand for what we truly believe and deserve. Quick to disrespect her but your mother? You will die for that woman you will ride for that woman, you cry for that woman, put your life aside for that woman. Use that same energy to the woman that can potentially be that mother to your child, your future. To all my women here's your recognition. You are strong, you are intelligent, you are capable of building an empire, simply because pussy is POWER.

To pops

Society makes it a trend to be fatherless, just like baby daddy drama and Father's Day memes. But you my old man never cared about what's trending or what's new. You cared about what you can do. You provided more than materialistic things , you provided your presence and that is enough for me. Despite the days your demons make you feel as though you don't give enough, you are enough. A blessing to be your child. Such an old soul, educated us, advised us , sacrificed for us .Unconditional love. Patience. Strength. Drive. The only man who hasn't disappointed me. Showing loyalty towards my mother and handing her happiness means everything. That's the kind of love I'd expect for myself, thanks to you I

will not settle for anything
less than I deserve.
My gratitude.
My appreciation.
My love.
And to those who are
fatherless does not mean
you are less...Loved. They
lacked the vision of their
fulfilling future due to
selfishness and
irresponsibility. No one's
loss but their own. Gain for
your descendants what you
couldn't receive.
You have been for yourself
who you truly need.
Be proud.

Friend

Friend.
A person whom one knows
and with whom one has a
bond of mutual affection.
One who can keep your
darkest and brightest parts
and store them in a place
temptation cannot
withhold.
An individual needing no
confirmation nor constant
communication to be
reassured that they are
appreciated and/or
remaining relevant.
A soul that shares common
interests as well as
personality differences.
A person who is there
through the bad as well as
the good no needing to
count favors.
Someone you never have to
question and the
comfortability remains.
One who is not biological
but close enough to
rename.
Family.
Thank you for being you.

Only we to see

I Hope you listened
although there's no sound. I
hope you felt although you
were not physically
touched. I hope you were
inspired and motivated to
express yourself although
it's just me. It's more than
ink on paper, it's poetry.
You took the time to read
now write your soul on
paper for only we to see. If
you would like to show your
creativity take a photo and
tag me on IG .
Keepinupwith_mari

About the author

Poet, Marianna Drunnamanio, born and raised in Hartford, Connecticut; has been writing poetry since elementary. Inspired by Grammy nominated singer/songwriter and poet, Jhene Aiko Efuru Chilombo, She has converted her poems into a short poetry book in hopes to continue to inspire and motivate her readers with both relatable content and spoken words. She also performs her poetry at poetry slams and other poetry events giving audiences a genuine feel of her powerful words.

Peace. Love. Happiness.

www.ingramcontent.com/pod-product-compliance
Ingram Content Group UK Ltd.
Pitfield, Milton Keynes, MK11 3LW, UK
UKHW020235250726
13967UKWH00001B/381

9 781794 859647